The Description of

The Believing Man and Believing Woman

Dhū 'l-Nūn al-Miṣri

Cover design: Salim Abul Salihat

Printed in the United States of America.

First Edition.

ISBN 979-8-9898696-1-9

Origem Publishing.

Contents

Introduction

"The Description of the Believing Man and Woman," authored by Dhū 'l-Nūn al-Miṣri is an early religious text that delves into the characteristics and virtues of the believer in Islam. The text, rich in linguistic nuances and primarily referencing ideal attributes rather than directly quoting primary religious scriptures, offers a detailed description of the characteristics of a believing man and woman.

The text presents the believing man as embodying humility, patience, wisdom, a strong ethical foundation, and a profound connection to God. In a similar vein, it portrays the believing woman as self-aware, deeply faithful, and characterized by modesty in both behavior and speech. Key virtues such as generosity, forgiveness, modesty, and a relentless quest for knowledge and understanding are emphasized. This work interweaves spirituality, ethical conduct, and the quest for knowledge, depicting how a believer navigates life's trials while steadfastly rooted in faith and virtue.

Preceded by a brief biography of the author, this translation serves not only as a spiritual guide and a bilingual instructional resource but also opens a window to ideas promulgated in the early Islamic period related to both spirituality, philosophy, and tradition. To add to the value of the book, I also translated a poem that was said by Dhū 'l-Nūn on the topic of eternal praise and divine majesty.

Joe W. Bradford

Biography of Dhū 'l-Nūn al-Miṣri

His name and lineage

His name was Thawbān ibn Ibrāhīm, known as Dhū 'l-Nūn, Abu al-Fayḍ al-Miṣri. He was born in 180 AH / 796 AD in Akhmīm, Upper Egypt.

One of four boys, he was the only one of his father's children to take the path he took. His father was of Nubian origin, a former client (mawlā) of Isḥāq ibn Muḥammad al-Anṣārī, who was from the narrators found in Sunan Abī Dawūd.

Known for his eloquence, he was held in high regard by all those he visited. He visited Damascus, Antioch, Mecca, and Medina, and resided with the Ascetics (zuhhād) and Hadithists (muḥaddithīn) in all those places. He was forcibly taken to Iraq twice and visited Baghdad as well as Samarra while there.

His teachers and students

Dhū 'l-Nūn narrated from Mālik, Layth, Sufyān ibn 'Uyayna, Fuḍayl ibn 'Iyāḍ, 'Abdullah Ibn Lahī'a, and others. Al-Daraquṭnī did not hold his ḥadīth from Mālik in high regard, nevertheless he was known as a pious worshiper ('Ābid Ṣāliḥ) as Ibn Asakir mentioned. Al-Dhahabi said "...he narrated few ḥadīth and was not precise." Ibn Yūnus said about him "He was an eloquent, wise, scholar." Al-Jawzaqāni said, "He was an ascetic, weak in ḥadīth."[1]

His students include al-Junayd ibn Muḥammad (the famous ascetic), Miqdām ibn Dāwūd al-Ru'aynī, Aḥmad ibn Ṣubayh al-Fayyūmī, and others.[2]

---

[1] Lisān al-Mīzān, 3/438.

[2] See: Siyar 'Alām al-Nubalā' 22/143, al-Nujūm al-Zāhira 1/157, Tārīkh Dimashq 17/419, Wafayāt al-'A'yān 1/101, and Ḥilyat al-Awliyā 9/331.

His beliefs and mysticism

Dhū 'l–Nūn's beliefs were those of Ahl al–Sunna, adhering to the beliefs of the Salaf, the earliest generations of this Ummah, in the areas of worship, divine attributes, and following the Sunna. Anyone who reads his biography in the earliest works that mention him, can see this clearly, especially in the poems that Abu Nu'aym relates from him in his Ḥilyat al–Awliyā'.[3] While there is not sufficient space to mention all these texts, here are a number of his statements on issues of creed that exhibit this.

- About the Quran he said, "The Quran is Allah's speech, uncreated."[4]

- About divine attributes and anthropomorphism, "Whatever you imagine in your mind, God is different from that."[5]

---

[3] For one such example, see the addendum to this book on page ??.

[4] Siyar 'Alām al–Nubalā' 11/534.

[5] Tārīkh al–Islām of al–Dhahabi, 18/168.

- About worship, character, and following the Sunna he said, "Corruption has entered into creation due to six things: Firstly: Weakness of intention in the deeds for the Hereafter. Secondly: Their bodies became captive to their desires. Thirdly: Long hopes despite the nearness of death. Fourthly: Preferring the satisfaction of created beings over the satisfaction of the Creator. Fifthly: Following their whims and discarding the Sunna of their Prophet ﷺ behind their backs. And sixthly: They use the minor faults of the predecessors as an excuse for themselves and bury their many virtues."[6]

- On his alignment with the 'Aqīda of the Salaf, Abu Bakr al-Marwazi said, "I entered upon Dhū 'l-Nūn in prison while we were in the camp. He said to me: How is our masterﷻs condition? - referring to Ahmad ibn Hanbal."[7]

---

[6] Al-Ghunya li Ṭālibī 'l-Ḥaqq of al-Jaylāni, Pg. 2/309.

[7] Manāqib al-Imam Aḥmad, Pg.162.

Despite these statements and others, he was accused of heresy two times in his life. Once after the ascension of the 'Abbasid Caliph al-Wāthiq in the year 227H/842CE during the Fitna surrounding the Quran's "createdness." The Mu'tazila attacked him for holding to the orthodox view that Qur'an was Allah's word and therefore uncreated.

Later in life, and despite his orthodox views on Allah's attributes, he was attacked again by the Mālikiyya in Egypt, chief amongst them 'Abdullah ibn 'Abd 'l-Hakam, this time for teaching things such as spiritual states and conditions, and the stations of the Awliyā'. The "mysticism" in question seems to be based on gnosis (ma'rifa), often meaning a more personal spiritual understanding of faith beyond rational and textual proofs. This kind of knowledge suggests a direct and personal connection with the divine. From his more well-known statements on the topic is his saying, "The knower does not adhere to one state; rather, he adheres to the command of his Lord in all states."[8] To our modern sensibilities, this type of statement seems benign. However, the accusation of heresy here centers on such things being foreign to the Salaf and their vernacular.

Despite this, he still adhered to the principles of Ahl al-Sunna, maintaining alignment with the established orthodox beliefs and practices of the earliest generations of Islam. Al-Dhahabi said about him: "He was among those who were tested and harmed because he brought to them knowledge they were not accustomed to. He was the first to speak in Egypt about the arrangement of spiritual states and the stations of the saints, so the ignorant said: He is a heretic."[9] A few modern researchers remarked, "One may conclude that Dhū 'l-Nūn did not have any "systematic teaching about the mystic states (aḥwāl) and the stations of the mystic way

---

[8] See: Siyar 'Alām al-Nubalā' 11/536.

[9] Mīzān al-'itidāl, 2/33.

(maqāmāt)", but rather seems to have referred to the ethical, psychological and spiritual states of the mystic in various ways and from different points of view."[10]

His case was raised to the governor of Egypt, who asked him about his beliefs and was pleased with what he heard. He was then ordered to the court of al-Mutawakkil, who rose to power in 232H. Despite having ordered him killed, the caliph met him and then became infatuated with him, preferring him to the other ascetics (zuhhād). Dhū 'l-Nūn later returned to Egypt.

Despite enduring attacks and his name being cleared by the authorities, the stigma unjustly associated with him persisted until his death. However, following his passing, an extraordinary event occurred that altered public perception: birds were reportedly seen

---

[10] Ebstein, Michael. Dhū 'l-Nūn al-Miṣrī and Early Islamic Mysticism. Pg. 560 and 570, who references Smith, "Dhu'l-Nūn", EI2.

shading his funeral.[11] This unusual occurrence led the people of Egypt to reevaluate their stance, eventually leading to a posthumous shift in sentiment as they began to recognize and respect his true character and contributions.

A subsequent cult grew up around his personality, resulting in two developments. The first was an unwarranted veneration of his grave (which seems to have happened only after the late 4th century). The second is the attribution of a number of esoteric statements and fantastical stories to him in works from the 5th century onward without chains of oral transmission typical to earlier scholarship. Perhaps one cause for this is that Dhū 'l-Nūn's students are not known to have compiled his teachings, unlike some of his contemporaries.[12]

---

[11] Siyar 'Alām al-Nubalā' 11/533.

[12] Ebstein, Michael. Dhū 'l-Nūn al-Miṣrī and Early Islamic Mysticism. Pg. 560, 570, and 604–610.

Medieval Biographers mention that Dhū 'l-Nūn was also interested in ancient medicine and chemistry/Alchemy, and that he could read hieroglyphics. This should not be a surprise, given that Akhmīm (where he was born) and Giza (where he lived) were both centers for Coptic medicine and textiles. Some modern writers have used these reports to claim he was a "magician" and "theurgist," but these claims are baseless.[13]

---

[13] Ibid. Pg. 592.

His Death and Burial

Dhu 'l-Nūn died in 246 AH / 861 AD in Giza, Egypt. His funeral bier was carried over the water to the Lesser Qarāfa graveyard, out of fear that the crowds following it might damage the bridge between Giza and Fusṭāṭ (Medieval Cairo).[14] As mentioned previously, a flock of birds was seen shading the procession.

Before he died, and in accordance with the Sunna, Dhu 'l-Nūn ordered that his grave be leveled with the ground.[15]

---

[14] Ibid.

[15] Lisān al-Mīzān, 3/431.

The Provenance of This Text

This text is based on the Dār al-Bashā'ir print of the text, edited by the late Ramzy Sa'ad Dimashqiyya, may Allah have mercy on him. That edition is based on two main sources.

The first is a manuscript folio of the treatise found in the Ẓāhiriyya library of Damascus, now known as the Asad Library, in collection 3824, treatise number 12, in three pages (147–149) from the narration of Abu Dujāna Aḥmad ibn Ibrāhīm from Dhū 'l-Nūn al-Miṣri. It was written by 'Abd 'l-Raḥmān ibn Yūnus ibn Ibrāhīm al-Anṣārī al-Tūnisī. It includes marginalia indicating it was from the Waqf of Nūr 'l-Dīn 'Ali ibn Mas'ūd ibn Nafīs al-Mawṣili, as well as manuscript note showing it had been read in its entirety by Ibn Abd 'l-Hādi al-Ḥanbali (d. 856).

The second source contains only the first half of this treatise, that related to the believing man, is found in Ibn Asakir's Tarikh Dimashq (17/419) under the biography of Dhū 'l-Nūn.

The Text and its Translation

بِسْمِ اللهِ الرَّحْمٰنِ الرَّحِيْمِ

وصلَّى الله على سيدنا محمد و آله

قال أبو دجانة أحمد بن إبراهيم: قرأتُ على أبي الفيض ذي النون بن إبراهيم الإخميمي رحمه الله، قال:

With Allah's name, Beneficent, Merciful.

And may He bless and grace our master Muḥammad and his family Abu Dujāna Aḥmad ibn Ibrāhīm said: I read upon Abī 'l-Fayḍ, Dhū 'l-Nūn ibn Ibrāhīm al-Ikhmīmī, God have mercy on him, that he said:

صِفَةُ المُؤمِنِ.

بِشْرُهُ في وَجْهِهِ، و حُزنُهُ في قَلبِهِ. أوسَعُ شَيءٍ صَدْرَاً، و أذَلُّ شَيءٍ نَفْسَاً. زَجِرٌ عن كُلِّ آفَةٍ، حَاضِرٌ على كُلِّ حَسَن. لا حَقُودٌ، ولا حَسُودٌ. ولا وَثَّابٌ، ولا سَبَّابٌ. ولا عَيَّابٌ، ولا مُغْتَابٌ. يَكْرَهُ الرِّفْعَةَ، و يَشْنَأُ السُّمعَةَ.

The Description of the Believing Man.

His joy is in his face & his sorrow in his heart. He has the most open chest & most humbled soul. Abstinent from every harm, present for every good. Not envious or spiteful. He does not pummel nor curse. He does not chastise or backbite. He dislikes haughtiness and despises ostentation.

طَوِيلُ الغَمِّ، بَعِيدُ الهَمِّ. كَثِيرُ الصَّمْتِ، وَقُورٌ. ذَكُورٌ، صَبُورٌ، شَكُورٌ. مَعْمُورٌ بِفِكْرِهِ، مَسْرُورٌ بِفَقْرِهِ. سَهْلُ الخَلِيقَةِ، لَيِّنُ العَرِيكَةِ. كَثِيرُ الحَيَاءِ، صَيِّنُ الوَقَارِ، قَلِيلُ الأذَى. لا مُتَأَفِّكٌ، ولا مُتَهَتِّكٌ. إِنْ ضَحِكَ لم يُخْرَق، وإِنْ غَضِبَ لم يَنْزَق. ضَحِكُهُ تَبَسُّمٌ، واسْتِفْهَامُهُ تَعَلُّمٌ، وَ مُرَاجَعَتُهُ تَفَهُّمٌ. كَثِيرٌ عِلْمُهُ، عَظِيمٌ حِلْمُهُ. وَثِيقٌ عَزْمُهُ، كَثِيرٌ رُحْمُهُ.

His sorrow is long, and his worries reach far. His silence is much; He is dignified, evocative, patient, and grateful. Busied by his thoughts, elated by his poverty. He is easy going and soft handed. His modesty is strong, his dignity is protected, he harms little. He does not concoct falsehood or defend his own ego. If he laughs, he is not hysterical. If he is angered, he is not off kilter. His laughter is a smile, his inquiries are learning, and his review is for understanding. His knowledge is much, his forbearance great. His fortitude is solid, his benevolence is plenty.

لا يَبْخَلُ، ولا يَعْجَلُ. ولا يَضْجَرُ، ولا يَبْطَرُ. ولا يَحِيفُ في حُكمِهِ، ولا يَجُورُ في عِلْمِهِ. نِيَّتُهُ أَصْلَبُ مِنَ الحَجَرِ، و مُنَادَمَتُهُ أَحلى مِنَ الشَّهْدِ. لا خَشِعٌ، ولا هَلِعٌ. ولا عَنِفٌ، ولا صَلِفٌ. ولا مُتَعَمِّقٌ، ولا مُتَكَلِّفٌ. جَمِيلُ المَنَازَعَةِ، كَرِيْمُ المُرَاجَعَةِ. عَدْلٌ إِنْ غَضِبَ، رَقِيقٌ إِنْ طَلَبَ. لا مُتَهَوِّرٌ، ولا مُتَجَبِّرٌ. خَلِيصُ الوُدِّ، وَثِيقُ العَهْدِ، وَفِيُّ الوَعْدِ.

He is not stingy or hasty. He is not displeased [when going without a livelihood] or heavy handed [when gaining it back]. He does not overstep when ruling nor is he shaky in knowledge. His intention is harder than stone; his companionship is sweeter than honey. He is not debased or keyed up, not harsh or brash, not bloviated, or pretentious. Gracious in dispute, generous in recourse. He is not reckless or imperious. His love, unadulterated; his trusts, dependable; his promises, deliverable.

شَفِيقٌ، وَصُولٌ، حَلِيمٌ. حَمُولٌ، قَلِيلُ الفُضُولِ. رَاضٍ عَنِ الله -عَزَّ وجلَّ-، مُخَالِفٌ
لِهَوَاهُ. لَا يَغْلُظُ عَلَى مَنْ يُؤْذِيهِ، ولا يَخُوضُ فِيَا لا يَعْنِيهِ. إنْ سُبَّ بَدِيهاً لم يَسُبَّ،
وإنْ سَأَلَ و مُنِعَ لم يَغْضَب. لا يَشْمَتُ بِمُصِيبَةٍ، ولا يذْكُرُ أَحَداً بغِيبَةٍ. كَثِيرُ
الفَضْلِ، رَحِيبٌ. سَهْلٌ، لَيِّنُ الجَنَاحِ. صَدُوقُ اللِّسَانِ، عَفِيفُ الطَّمَعِ. خَفِيفُ
المَؤُونَةِ، كَثِيرُ المَعُونَةِ. وَرِعٌ عَنِ المُحَرَّمَاتِ، وَقَّافٌ عَنِ الشُّبُهَاتِ.

Caring, connected, forbearing, enduring; He wastes little [time]. He is pleased with God, opposing his own desires. He is not crude with those that harm him; he does not bother with what does not concern him. If he is cursed, he does not reciprocate; if he asks and is denied he does not get angry. He feels no schadenfreude for misfortune, nor does he libel others. He is abundant in virtue, welcoming. Easy going, soft sided. True of tongue, chaste of desires. He is not burdensome & is helpful in many ways. Cautious around unpermitted things, He avoids the questionable.

عَظِيمُ الشُّكْرِ عَلَى البَلَاءِ، طَوِيلُ الصَّبْرِ عَلَى الأَذَى. غَزِيرٌ خَيْرُهُ، قَلِيلٌ شَرُّهُ.

إِنْ سُئِلَ أَعْطَىٰ، وإِنْ ظُلِمَ عَفَا. وإِنْ مُنِعَ بَذَلَ، وإِنْ قُطِعَ وَصَلَ. مُمْتَحِنٌ لِقَلْبِهِ،

مُسْتَأْثِرٌ لِرَبِّهِ. أَدْمَثُ مِنَ الزُّبْدِ، وأَحْلَىٰ مِنَ الشَّهْدِ، وأَصْلَبُ مِنَ الصَّلْدِ. يَأْنَسُ مِنَ

البَلَاءِ بِمَا يَسْتَوْحِشُ مِنْهُ أَهْلُ الدُّنْيَا. أَمَّارٌ بِالحَقِّ، نَهَّاءٌ بِالصِّدْقِ. غَضَّابٌ للهِ، مُسْرِعٌ

في رِضَاهُ. قَادِحٌ لِعِلْمِهِ، مُزَوِّلٌ لأَمَلِهِ، مُنَزِّلٌ لأَجَلِهِ. قَدْ عَلِمَ هَوَانَ صِغَرِهِ، وَعَرَفَ

قَدْرَ نَفْسِهِ.

Immense is his gratitude for tribulations; long is his patience in face of harm. His good runs deep: his evil is scant. If asked he gives, if wronged he pardons. If denied he provides, if cut-off he connects. He examines his heart and gives his Lord [before others]. Softer than cream, sweeter than honey, more formidable than a boulder. He feels at home during hardships in the same way the people of this worldly life are disturbed by them. Ever-commanding rightfully; ever-forbidding truthfully. Ever-angry for God; ever-racing to His pleasure. Contemptuous of his own knowledge; debasing of his own hopes; recollecting his own expiry. He realizes the frailty of insignificance, recognizing his own stature.

فَشَنَأ كِبْرَهَا، و مَقَتَ عِزَّهَا. وَألْزَمَهَا كُلَّ ذِلَّةٍ، وبَوَّأَهَا كُلَّ مِهْنَةٍ. نَاصِرٌ لِلدِّينِ، مُحَامِ
عَنِ الْمُسْلِمِينَ، كَهْفٌ لِلْمَسَاكِينَ. لَا يَخْرِقُ الثَّنَاءُ سَمْعَهُ، ولَا يَنْكَأُ الطَّمَعُ قَلْبَهُ.
ولَا يَقْرَبُ الغَضَبُ حِلْمَهُ، ولَا يَظْلَعُ الجَهْلُ عِلْمَهُ، ولَا تُقِلُّ الْمُلِمَّاتُ عَزْمَهُ.
قَوَّالٌ، [عَمَّالٌ]. عَالِمٌ، حَازِمٌ. لَا بِفَحَّاشٍ، ولَا بِطَيَّاشٍ. هَؤُولٌ فِي غَيْرِ عُنْفٍ، بَذُولٌ
فِي غَيْرِ سَرَفٍ.

Due to this he rejects its pride & scorns it is ego. He adheres to its ever debasement & places it in ever trial. He is a victor of this Faith; a protector of Muslims; a cave for the poor. Praise pierces not his hearing; covetousness does not pull back the scab on his heart. Anger does not approach his forbearance; Scorn does not dislodge his awareness; Misfortunes do not faze his resilience. Outspoken; active; a scholar resolute. Not lewd or erratic. Imposing but without harm, openhanded but without being lavish.

كَثِيرٌ عِلْمُهُ، قَلِيلٌ جَهْلُهُ. لَا يَقْتَفِي أَثَراً، ولا يَحْتَقِرُ بَشَراً. رَفِيقٌ بالخَلْقِ، سَرَّاحٌ في الأَرْضِ. عَوْنٌ لِلضَّعيفِ، وغَوْثٌ للمَلْهُوفِ. لا يَهْتِكُ سِتْراً، ولا يَكْشِفُ سِرّاً. كَثِيرُ البَلْوَىٰ، قَلِيلُ الشَّكْوَىٰ. إِنْ رَأَى خَيْراً ذَكَرَهُ، وإِنْ عَلِمَ شَرّاً سَتَرَهُ. يَسْتُرُ العَيْبَ، [ويَحْفَظُ الغَيْبَ]. ويُقِيلُ العَثْرَةَ، ويَغْفِرُ الزَّلَّةَ. لَا يَطَّلِعُ على نُصْحٍ فَيَذَرَهُ، ولا يَرَىٰ جُنْحَ حُمُقٍ فَيَصِلَهُ.

His knowledge is much; is ignominy little. He does not follow up on missteps; he does not denigrate any human. Kind to creation; free on the earth. Aid to the weak; Succor to the aggrieved. He does not pull down curtains, nor reveal secrets. Much are his trials, yet little are his complaints. If he sees good, he mentions it; if he recognizes bad, he covers it. He conceals faults, preserves what is private, dismisses faux-pas and forgives missteps. He is never exposed to advice then leaves it and never senses from himself crudeness then continues it.

أَمِينٌ، [رَصِينٌ]. [نَقِيٌّ]، تَقِيٌّ. زَكِيٌّ، رَضِيٌّ. طَوِيلُ الصَّمتِ في غَيرِ عِيٍّ. يَقْبَلُ
العُذْرَ، وَيَحْمِلُ الذِّكْرَ. ويُحَسِّنُ بالنَّاسِ ظَنَّهُ، ويَتَّهِمُ على العَيْبِ نَفْسَهُ. يُحِبُّ في اللهِ
بِفِقْهِ و عِلْمٍ، ويَقْطَعُ في اللهِ بِحَزْمٍ وَ عَزْمٍ. ولا يَخْرَقُ بِهِ فَرَحٌ، ولا يَطِيشُ بِهِ [تَرَحٌ].
خِلْطَتُهُ فُرْجَةٌ، ورُؤْيَتُهُ حُجَّةٌ. صَفَّاهُ العِلْمُ مِنْ كُلِّ خُلُقٍ نَكِدٍ، كَمَا تُصَفِّي النَّارُ
خَبَثَ الحَدِيدِ.

Trustworthy, sober. Pure, mindful. Pious. Long in silence but not from impediment. He accepts excuses, elevates others. He has the best opinions of others and accuses his self of deficiency. He loves God with understanding & knowledge and cuts off for God with resolve & determination. He is not overpowered by exuberance or apathy. Mixing with him is a respite, seeing him is an evidence. Knowledge cleansed him of every base character, as fire purifies iron of slag.

لَا يُشِيرُ بِمِنَّةٍ، وَلَا يَمُنُّ بِنِعْمَةٍ. مُذَكِّرٌ لِلْغَافِلِ، مُعَلِّمٌ لِلْجَاهِلِ. لَا يُتَوَقَّعُ لَهُ بَائِقَةٌ، وَلَا يُخَافُ لَهُ غَائِلَةٌ. كُلُّ سَعْيٍ عِنْدَهُ أَصْلَحُ مِنْ سَعْيِهِ، وَكُلُّ نَفْسٍ عِنْدَهُ أَصْلَحُ مِنْ نَفْسِهِ. عَالِمٌ بِعَيْبِهِ، مَشْغُولٌ بِغَمِّهِ، لَا يُفِيقُ لِغَيْرِ رَبِّهِ. شَهِيدٌ، وَحِيدٌ. قَرِيبٌ، غَرِيبٌ. يُحِبُّ اللهَ، وَيُجَاهِدُ لِيَبْتَغِي رِضَاهُ. وَلَا يَنْتَقِمُ لِنَفْسِهِ، وَلَا يُوَالِي فِي سَخَطِ رَبِّهِ. مُخَالِطٌ لِأَهْلِ الذِّكْرِ، مُجَالِسٌ لِأَهْلِ الصِّدْقِ، مُؤْثِرٌ لِأَهْلِ الْحَقِّ.

He does not point out his kindnesses or remind of his favors. He reminds the heedless & teaches the ignorant. Distress is not expected from him, or vexation feared from him. Everyone else's efforts are better than his Every soul in his opinion is better than his own. He knows his faults, preoccupied by his own worries; he does not awake but for his Lord. A witness: he stands alone. Close yet estranged. He loves God and strives to seek out His pleasure. He does not take revenge for himself and does not show affinity that would earn his Lord's wrath. He mixes with the people of remembrance; He sits with the people of honesty. He defers to the people of truth.

عَوْنٌ لِلغَرِيبِ، أَبٌ لِلْيَتِيم. بَعْلٌ لِلأَرْمَلَةِ، حَفِيٌّ بِأَهلِ المَسْكَنَةِ. مَرْجُوٌّ لِكُلِّ كُرْبَةٍ، مَأْمُولٌ لِكُلِّ شِدَّةٍ. هَشَّاشٌ، بَشَّاشٌ. لا بِعَبَّاسٍ، ولا جَسَّاسٍ. مُحِبٌّ، صَادِقٌ. كَظَّامٌ، بَسَّامٌ. دَقِيقُ النَّظَرِ، عَظِيمُ الخَطَرِ. جَائِلٌ مُمَلْمَلٌ، سَاكِنٌ مُقَلْقَلٌ. مَعْرُوفٌ في أَرضِهِ، غَرِيبٌ في أَهلِهِ، مُبغَضٌ في جَمْعِهِ.

مغيث.

رَحِمَهُ اللهُ.

A helper to the stranger; a father to the orphan; A husband to the widow; soft soled with the poor. He is hoped for in every distress, longed for in every hardship. Welcoming and smiling. Not frowning or shifty-eyed. Beloved, truthful. Withholding his anger, constantly smiling. Particular in analysis, great in stature. Motivated in meaning, calm yet active. Well-known in his land, a stranger among his people, envied in gatherings.

A helper.

God have mercy on him.

صِفَةُ المُؤْمِنَةِ.

نَاظِرَةٌ فِي عَيْبِهَا، مُفَكِّرَةٌ فِي ذَنْبِهَا، مُقْبِلَةٌ على رَبِّهَا. خَفِيٌّ صَوْتُها، كَثِيرٌ صَمْتُهَا. لَيِّنَةُ الجَنَاحِ، عَفِيفَةُ اللِّسانِ. ظَاهِرَةُ الحَيَاءِ، وَرِعَةٌ عن الخَنَاءِ. وَاسِعَةُ الصَّدرِ، عَظِيمَةُ الصَّبْرِ. قَلِيلَةُ المَكرِ، كَثِيرَةُ الشُّكْرِ. نَقِيَّةُ الجَيْبِ، طَاهِرَةٌ مِنَ العَيْبِ. حَيِيَّةٌ، كَرِيمَةٌ. رَضِيَّةٌ، زَكِيَّةٌ. رَزِينَةٌ، نَجِيبَةٌ .

The Description of the Believing Woman.

Observant of her deficiency, concerned about her sin, preceding to her Lord. Her voice is hushed, she is long in silence. Her wings are lowered; her tongue is chaste. Her shyness is manifest, she is abstinent from indecency. Her chest is expansive, her patience is immense. Her plots are few, her gratitude is profuse. Her pockets are empty, she is cleansed of defects. She is bashful and generous. Satisfied and pure; Dignified and magnanimous.

سَهْلَةُ الخُلُقِ، رَقِيقَةٌ، رَفِيقَةٌ. بَرِيَّةٌ مِنَ الكَذِبِ، نَقِيَّةٌ مِنَ العُجْبِ. تَارِكَةٌ لِلقَذَىٰ، زَاهِدَةٌ في الدُّنيَا. سَاكِنَةٌ، حَازِمَةٌ. سَتِّيرَةٌ، خَفِرَةٌ. لا مُتَفَاكِهَةٌ، ولا مُتَهَتِّكَةٌ. قَلِيلَةُ الحِيَلِ، وَثِيقَةُ العَمَلِ. رَحِيمَةُ القَلْبِ، خَلِيصَةُ الوُدِّ. إنْ زُجِرَتِ انْزَجَرَت، وإنْ أُمِرَتِ ائْتَمَرَت. تَشْنَأُ الصَّلَفَ، وتَبْغُضُ السَّرَفَ. وتَكْرَهُ المَكْرُوهَ، وتَمْقُتُ الفَخْرَ .

Her character is relaxed, soft, and friendly. Absolved of dishonesty, free of ostentation. She leaves off the small stuff, ascetic in this life. She is tranquil and resolute. Extremely modest and demure. She wastes no time with frivolity and levity. Her tricks are few; she cherishes her good deeds. Her heart is merciful, her love is unadulterated. If admonished she accepts, if ordered she follows through. She rejects harshness and hates wastefulness. She dislikes what is discouraged & hates pompousness.

وَتَتَفَقَّدُ نَفْسَهَا بِطِيبِ النِّسَاءِ: الكُحْلِ والمَاءِ. قَنُوعٌ بِالكَفَافِ، واستِتَارٌ بِالعَفَافِ. لَهَا رَحْمَةٌ بِالأَهْلِ، ورِفْقٌ بِالبَعْلِ. تَضَعُ لَهُ خَدَّهَا، وتُخْلِصُ لَهُ وُدَّهَا. وتُمَلِّكُهُ نَفْسَهَا، ولا تَمْلأُ مِنْهُ طَرْفَهَا. وتَتْرُكُ لأَمْرِهِ أَمْرَهَا، وتُخْرِج لآرائِهِ رَأْيَهَا. وتُوَكِّلُهُ عَلَى نَفْسِهَا، وتَأْمَنُهُ عَلَى سِرِّهَا. وتُصْفِيهِ غَايَةَ الحُبِّ، وتُؤْثِرُهُ عَلَى الأُمِّ والأَبِّ. لا تَلْفِظُ بِعَيْبِهِ، ولا تُخْبِرُ بِسِرِّهِ. تُحَسِّنُ أَمْرَهُ، وتَتَبَّعُ سُرُورَهُ. ولا تَجْفُوهُ في عُسْرِهِ، ولا تَقْلاهُ في فَقْرِهِ.

She applies to herself a women's fragrance: water & antimony. She is satisfied with sufficiency, covered by her chastity. Merciful with family, kind with her husband. She lends him her cheek and devotes her love to him. She gives herself to him and cannot get enough of seeing him. She defers her command to his and lay out her opinion to him. She trusts him with her life and entrusts him with her secret. She pours out for him the purest of love, preferring him over mother and father. She speaks not of his deficiencies and tells no one of his secrets. She beautifies his situation, seeking his joy. She does not put him down in hard times nor forsake him during poverty.

بَلْ تَزِيدُ فِي الفَقْرِ وُدّاً، وعَلَى الافْتِقَارِ حُبّاً. تَلْقَى غَضَبَهُ بِحِلْمٍ وصَبْرٍ، وتَلْقَى مُعَاشَرَتَهُ بِوُدٍّ و شُكْرٍ. إنْ أَسَاءَ إلَيْهَا غَفَرَتْ، وإنْ آثَرَ عَلَيْهَا صَبَرَتْ. تَتَرَضَّاهُ فِي غَضَبِهِ، وتَتَوقَّاهُ فِي سَخَطِهِ. وتَسْتَوْحِشُ لِغَيْبَتِهِ، وتَسْتَأْنِسُ لِرُؤْيَتِهِ.

Instead, her affection increases with poverty and her love with need. She meets his anger with forbearance and patience and matches companionship with love and gratitude. If he wrongs her, she forgives; if he overlooks her, she is patient. She pleases him when angry and dedicated to him when upset. She misses him deeply when absent and finds pleasure in seeing him.

قَدْ فَهِمتْ عَنِ الله ذِكْرَهُ وَعِلْمَهُ، فَقَامَت فِيهِ بِحَقِّ فَضْلِهِ. فَعَظُمَ بِذَلِكَ فَاقتُهَا
إِليهِ، ولَمْ تَجْعَلْ لها مُعَوَّلاً إلَّا عَلَيْهِ. فَهُوَ لَهَا سَمْعٌ ولُبٌّ، وهِيَ لَهُ بَصَرٌ وقَلْبٌ.

رحمها الله من مؤمنة.

She understands from God his remembrance and knowledge, so stands for his virtue truthfully. She grows with this in her desire of him, not placing another for herself to depend on. So, he is – for her – hearing and consciousness, and she is – for him – eyesight and heart.

God have mercy on her, what a believer.

{16}

تَمَّت والحمد لله وحده وصلواته على خير خلقه محمد وآله ، كتب عبد الرحمن
بن يونس التونسى مصلِّيًا ومسلِّمًا.

With this it is complete, and all praise is due Allah alone with
blessings sent upon the best of His creation Muḥammad and his
family. Transcribed by 'Abd 'l-raḥmān ibn Yūnus al-Tūnisī, with
blessings and prayers.

انتهـى كلامـه رحمـه الله والحمـد لله الـذي بنعمتـه تـتم الصـالحات انتهيـت مـن ترجمـة هـذا الكتـاب ليلـة الجمعـة لخمـس ليـال مضـت من شهر جمادى الأولى سنة ١٤٤٣،

وكتبه: أبو لقمان (جو برادفورد) الأمريكي.

The author's words are complete, may Allah have mercy on him. And All praises are due to Allah, who through His blessings good deeds are completed. I completed the translation of this book on Friday evening, five nights into Jumada al-Ula, 1443.

Signed, Abu Luqmān Joe Bradford al-Amrīkī.

Addendum:

An Ode of Eternal Praise and Divine Majesty

The poem attributed to Dhū 'l-Nūn covers several themes. It opens with boundless praise for Allah, emphasizing His omnipotence, omniscience, and transcendence, yet noting His involvement in the natural world. The poem depicts natural and cosmic phenomena as reflections of Allah's power and delves into themes of death, judgment, and the hope for mercy, along with prayers for forgiveness and guidance.

It highlights human reliance on Allah's grace and mercy and concludes by depicting all creation, including angels and natural elements, in praise of Allah. This illustrates universal worship and weaves together Islamic concepts of Allah's greatness, the universe, and the believer's spiritual journey.

I named this poem the title "An Ode of Eternal Praise and Divine Majesty" specifically for publication, reflecting the poem's content. This title was not used by the original author or anyone else.

This poem is narrated by Abu Nuʿaym in his Ḥilyat al-Awliyāʾ, who narrates it through Ijāza from Abu Bakr ibn Aḥmad al-Baghdādi as well as through Samāʿ from ʿUthmān ibn Muḥammad al-ʿUthmāni, from Muḥammad ibn Abd ʾl-Malik ibn Hāshim, from Dhū ʾl-Nūn. It is also found in Muhammad ibn Aydamur al-Mustaʿṣimi's (d.710 H) Al-Durr Al-Farīd wa Bayt Al-Qaṣīd in summary form without a chain of narration.[16]

---

[16] Al-Durr Al-Farīd wa Bayt Al-Qaṣīd 2/11.

قَالَ أَبُو نُعَيْمٍ فِي الحِلْيَةِ:

أَخْبَرَنَا أَبُو بَكْرِ بْنُ أَحْمَدَ الْبَغْدَادِيُّ، - فِي كِتَابِهِ وَقَدْ رَأَيْتُهُ - وَحَدَّثَنِي عَنْهُ عُثْمَانُ بْنُ
مُحَمَّدٍ الْعُثْمَانِيُّ، قَالَ: أَنْشِدْنِي مُحَمَّدُ بْنُ عَبْدِ الْمَلِكِ بْنِ هَاشِمٍ لِذِي النُّونِ بْنِ إِبْرَاهِيمَ
الْمِصْرِيِّ رَحِمَهُ اللَّهُ تَعَالَى:

Abu Nu'aym says[17]:

Abu Bakr ibn Aḥmad al-Baghdādī informed us – in his book
which I have seen – and 'Uthmān ibn Muḥammad al-'Uthmāni told me
about it. He said: Muḥammad ibn 'Abd 'l-Malik ibn Hāshim recited to
me from Dhū 'l-Nūn ibn Ibrāhīm al-Miṣri, may Allah have mercy on
him:

---

[17] Ḥilyat al-Awliyā' 9/388.

حَمْدًا يَفُوتُ مَدَى الْإِحْصَاءِ وَالْعَدَدِ	❁	الْحَمْدُ لِلَّهِ حَمْدًا لَا نَفَادَ لَهُ	1
حَمْدًا كَثِيرًا كَإِحْصَاءِ الْوَاحِدِ الصَّمَدِ	❁	وَيُعْجِزُ اللَّفْظَ وَالْأَوْهَامَ مَبْلَغُهُ	2
وَوَزْنَهُنَّ وَضِعْفُ الضِّعْفِ فِي الْعَدَدِ	❁	مِلْءَ السَّمَوَاتِ وَالْأَرَضِينَ مُذْ خُلِقَتْ	3
بَعْدَ الْقِيَامَةِ أَوْ يَفْنَى مَدَى الْأَبَدِ	❁	وَضِعْفُ مَا كَانَ وَمَا قَدْ يَكُونُ إِلَى	4
وَمَا اخْتَفَى فِي سَمَاءٍ أَوْ ثَرَى جُرْدِ	❁	وَضِعْفُ مَا دَارَتِ الشَّمْسُ الشُّرُوقَ	5

1 – All praise be to Allah, praise that knows no bounds,

   Praise that exceeds the limits of counting and number.

2 – A praise that eludes the grasp of words and imaginations,

   Abundant praise, as infinite as the One, the Eternal.

3 – Filling the heavens and the earth since their creation,

   And their weight, and twice as much in number.

4 – And twice as much as what has been and what will be,

   Until after the Resurrection, or until the end of eternity.

5 – And twice as much as what the rising sun has illuminated,

   And what has hidden in the sky or in the barren land.

وَكُلِّ نَفْسَةِ نَفْسٍ وَاكْتِسَابِ يَدِ	۞	وَضِعْفُ أَنْعُمِهِ فِي كُلِّ جَارِحَةٍ	6
مِنَ الهُدَى وَلَطِيفِ الصُّنْعِ وَالرَّفَدِ	۞	شُكْرًا لِمَا خَصَّنَا مِنْ فَضْلِ نِعْمَتِهِ	7
وَهُوَ المُحِيطُ بِنَا فِي كُلِّ مُرْتَصَدِ	۞	رَبِّ تَعَالَى فَلَا شَيْءَ يُحِيطُ بِهِ	8
وَلَا يُحَدُّ بِمِقْدَارٍ وَلَا أَمَدِ	۞	لَا الْأَيْنَ وَالْحَيْثُ وَالْكَيْفُ يُدْرِكُهُ	9
وَلَيْسَ لَهُ فِي الْمِثْلِ مِنْ أَحَدِ	۞	وَكَيْفَ يُدْرِكُهُ حَدٌّ وَلَمْ تَرَهُ عَيْنٌ	10

6 – And twice the blessings in every creature,

    In every breath and in the gains of every hand.

7 – Grateful for the special grace of His blessings,

    For His guidance, delicate crafting, and benefaction.

8 – My Lord is the Most High, nothing encompasses Him,

    And He encompasses us in every watchful moment.

9 – Neither place nor manner nor circumstance can comprehend Him,

    Nor is He limited by measure or by time.

10 – How can a limit perceive Him when no eye has seen Him,

    And He has no equal or likeness.

وَقَدْ تَعَالَى عَنِ الْأَشْبَاهِ وَالْوَلَدِ	❂	أَمْ كَيْفَ يَبْلُغُهُ وَهْمٌ بِلَا شَبَهِ	11
مِنْ غَيْرِ شَيْءٍ قَدِيمٍ كَانَ فِي الْأَبَدِ	❂	مَنْ أَنْشَأَ قَبْلَ الْكَوْنِ مُبْتَدِعًا	12
بِمَا يَشَاءُ فَلَمْ يَنْقُصْ وَلَمْ يَزِدِ	❂	وَدَهَرَ الدَّهْرَ وَالْأَوْقَاتَ وَاخْتَلَفَتْ	13
فِي الْكَوْنِ سُبْحَانَهُ مِنْ قَاهِرٍ صَمَدِ	❂	إِذْ لَا سَمَاءٌ وَلَا أَرْضٌ وَلَا شَبَحٌ	14
وَلَا يُرِيدُ بِهِمْ دَفْعًا لِمُضْطَهِدِ	❂	مَا ازْدَادَ بِالْخَلْقِ مُلْكًا حِينَ أَنْشَأَهُمْ	15

11- Or how can a thought reach Him, with no resemblance,

    Exalted is He, above likeness, and progeny.

12- He who originated creation from nothing before existence,

    Timelessly eternal, existing since forever.

13- He rent time asunder and the seasons change

    at His will, without decrease or increase.

14- When there was no sky, no earth, no form,

    Glorified is He, the Overpowering, the Eternal.

15- He did not increase in kingship by creating creation,

    Nor does He need them to repel oppression.

وَالْخَلْقُ تُضطَرُّ بِالتَّصْرِيفِ وَالْأَوَدِ	❁	وَكَيْفَ وَهُوَ غَنِيٌّ لَا افْتِقَارَ بِهِ	16
عَجْزًا عَلَى سُرْعَةٍ مِنْهُ وَلَا تُؤَدِ	❁	وَلَمْ يَدَعْ خَلْقَ مَا لَمْ يُبْدِ خَلْقَتَهُ	17
أَحْصَى بِهَا كُلَّ مَوْجُودٍ وَمُفْتَقَدِ	❁	إِحَاطَةً بِجَمِيعِ الْغَيْبِ عَنْ قَدَرِ	18
إِلَى فَوَاضِلِهِ فِي كُلِّ مُعْتَمَدِ	❁	وَكُلُّهُمْ بِافْتِقَارِ الْفَقْرِ مُعْتَرِفٌ	19
وَمَا عَادَ مِنْهُ وَمَا يَمْضِي فَلَمْ يَعُدِ	❁	الْعَالِمُ الشَّيْءَ فِي تَصْرِيفِ حَالَتِهِ	20

16- And how, when He is self-sufficient, not needing anything,

    While creation is in dire need of His management and kindness.

17- He did not leave off creating what He had not yet created,

    Due to inability, but at His own pace.

18- He encompasses all of the unseen, precisely,

    Counting every existent and missing thing.

19- And all recognize their absolute need for His excess,

    In every relied upon matter.

20- He knows the state of every single thing,

    What has passed from it, what remains, and what will not return.

وَمَا يَخْفَى عَلَيْهِ خَفِيٌّ جَالَ فِي خَلَدِ	❊	وَيَعْلَمُ السِّرَ مِنْ نَجْوى الْقُلُوبِ	21
مَدَارِجَ الذَّرِّ فِي صَفْوَانِهِ الجُلْدِ	❊	وَيَسْمَعُ الحِسَّ مِنْ كُلِّ الْوَرَى وَيَرَى	22
تَحْتَ الثَّرَى وَقَرَارِ الْغَمِّ وَالثَّمَدِ	❊	وَمَا تَوَارَى مِنَ الْأَبْصَارِ فِي ظُلَمِ	23
يَعْزُبْ وَلَمْ يَدَّكِرْ قُرْبٌ وَلَا بُعْدِ	❊	الْأَوَّلُ الْآخَرُ الْفَرْدُ الْمُهَيْمِنُ لَمْ	24
وَلَمْ يَزَلْ أَزَلِيًّا غَيْرَ ذِي فَقَدِ	❊	عَالٍ عَلِيٌّ عَلِيمٌ لَا زَوَالَ لَهُ	25

21- And He knows the secret whispers of hearts,

   Nothing hidden remains hidden from His knowledge.

22- He hears every sound from all creation, and sees,

   The paths of the smallest particles in His sturdy crystals.

23- And what is hidden from sight in darkness,

   Beneath the earth and in the depths of despair and darkness.

24- The First, the Last, the Unique, the Dominant,

   Nothing escapes Him, no distance or proximity.

25- Exalted, Supreme, All-Knowing, never ceasing,

   Timelessly eternal, without loss or need.

وَعَنْ مَقَالِ ذِي الشَّكِّ وَالْإِلْحَادِ	❁	وَجَلَّ فِي الْوَصْفِ عَنْ كُنْهِ الصِّفَاتِ	26
وَلَمْ يَنَلْهُ بِمَدْحٍ وَصْفُ مُجْتَهِدِ	❁	مَنْ لَا يُجَازَى بِنُعْمَى مِنْ فَوَاضِلِهِ	27
بِمَدْحِهِ لَمْ تَنَلْ إِلَّا إِلَى الْأَبَدِ	❁	وَكُلُّ فِكْرَةِ مَخْلُوقٍ إِذَا اجْتَهَدَتْ	28
لَمْ تَدْرِ مَا غَيْرُهُ رَبًّا وَلَمْ تَجِدِ	❁	مُسَبَّحٌ بِلُغَاتِ الْعَارِفَاتِ بِهِ	29
مَا تَقَاذَفَ بِالْأَمْوَاجِ وَالزَّبَدِ	❁	الْفَالِقُ النُّورَ وَالظَّلْمَاءَ وَهْيَ عَلَى	30

26- He is beyond description in His attributes,

    Beyond the words of those who doubt, deny, or resist.

27- No one can repay His favors with gratitude,

    And no praise by the striving can encompass Him.

28- Every thought of a creature, even if it strives,

    In praising Him, reaches only to the boundless.

29- Glorified by the languages of those who know Him,

    They do not know any other lord and do not find.

30- He split the light and darkness, while they,

    Tossed by the waves and the foam.

فَسَبَّحَتْ وَهْيَ فَوْقَ الْمَاءِ فِي مَيَدِ	❁	إِذَا مَدَّهَا فَوْقَ الرِّيحِ مُنْشِئُهَا	31
أَرْكَانَهَا بِشِدَادِ الصَّخْرِ وَالْجَلَدِ	❁	وَشَدَّهَا بِالْجِبَالِ الصُّمِّ فَاضْطَأَدَتْ	32
سَبْعًا طِبَاقًا بِلَا عَوْنٍ وَلَا عُمُدِ	❁	بَرَا السَّمَوَاتِ سَقْفًا ثُمَّ أَنْشَأَهَا	33
وَكُلُّ ذَلِكَ لَمْ يَثْقُلْ وَلَمْ يَؤُدِ	❁	تُقِلُّهُنَّ مَعَ الْأَرَضِينَ قُدْرَتُهُ	34
مِنَ الْخَلَائِقِ مِنْ مَثْنَى وَمِنْ وَهَدِ	❁	وَبَثَّ فِيهَا صُنُوفًا مِنْ بَدَائِعِهِ	35

31- When He spread them above the wind, their Creator,

    They glorified Him while above the water in their course.

32- And anchored them with immovable mountains,

    Their foundations strengthened by firm rock and resilience.

33- He created the heavens as a canopy, then established them,

    Seven layers, without aid or pillars.

34- His power upholds them along with the earths,

    All of that without burden or weariness.

35- And scattered therein varieties of His wonders,

    Among the creatures, in pairs and alone.

أَشْبَاحَهُ بَيْنَ مَكْسُورٍ وَمُنْجَرِدِ	❁	مِنْ كُلِّ جِنْسٍ بَرَا أَصْنَافَهُ وَذَرَا	36
لَا يَسْأَمُونَ لِطُولِ الدَّهْرِ وَالْأَمَدِ	❁	فِيهَا الْمَلَائِكُ بِالتَّسْبِيحِ خَاضِعَةٌ	37
كَالثَّوْرِ وَالنَّسْرِ وَالْإِنْسَانِ وَالْأَسَدِ	❁	فَمِنْهُمْ تَحْتَ سُوقِ الْعَرْشِ أَرْبَعَةٌ	38
فِي الْخَلْقِ بِالْعِيشَةِ الْمُرْضِيَّةِ الرَّغَدِ	❁	فَكُلُّ ذِي خِلْقَةٍ يَدْعُو لِمُشْبِهِهِ	39
تَجْرِينَ مِنْ فَلَكِ الْأَفْلَاكِ فِي كَبَدِ	❁	بَرَا السَّمَاءَ بُرُوجًا مِنْ كَوَاكِبِهَا	40

36- Of every kind He created its species and scattered,

    Its forms between the broken and the unadorned.

37- Therein the angels, humbly engaged in constant praise,

    Never tiring through the long stretch of time.

38- Among them, under the Throne's legs, four,

    Like the bull, the eagle, the human, and the lion.

39- Each creature prays for its kind in creation,

    For a life pleasing and comfortable.

40- He adorned the sky with constellations of its stars,

    Moving in the orbits within the expanse.

وَالْقُطْبُ فِي مَرْكَزٍ مِنْهُنَّ كَالْوَتَدِ	❈	مِنْهَا جِوَارٍ وَمِنْهَا رَاكِدٌ أَبَدًا	41
قَذْفِ الشَّيَاطِينِ مِنْ جِنَّاتِهَا الْمُرُدِ	❈	وَالشُّهْبُ تُحْرَقُ فِيهَا يَبْنِينَ إِلَى	42
مِنْهَا شِهَابُ نُجُومٍ دَائِمُ الرَّصَدِ	❈	وَكُلُّ مُسْتَرِقٍ لِلسَّمْعِ يَتْبَعُهُ	43
فِيهَا الصَّوَاعِقَ بَيْنَ الْمَاءِ وَالْبَرَدِ	❈	وَيَرْفَعُ الْغَيْمَ إِعْصَارُهَا فَتَرَى	44
يُحْيِي بِهِ كُلَّ ذِي رُوحٍ وَذِي جَسَدِ	❈	عَلَى هَوَاءٍ رَقِيقٍ فِي لَطَافَتِهِ	45

41 – Among them are satellites, and some forever stationary,

    And the pole in its center, like a peg.

42 – And meteors burning therein, aiming at,

    The devils from its rebellious jinn.

43 – And every eavesdropper followed by,

    A persistent meteor from its stars.

44 – And its hurricanes lift the clouds, and you see,

    In them thunderbolts between water and hail.

45 – On a gentle air in its subtlety,

    Reviving every living being and body.

مِنْهُ وَلَا هَرَبٌ إِلَى سَنَدِ	❈	وَصَيَّرَ الْمَوْتَ فَوْقَ الْخَلْقِ لَا لَجَأً	46
وَجْهَ الْإِلَهِ الْكَرِيمِ الدَّائِمِ الصَّمَدِ	❈	فَالْمَوْتُ مَيِّتٌ وَكُلُّ هَالِكُونَ خَلَا	47
كَعُمْرِ نُوحٍ وَلُقْمَانَ أَخِي لَبَدِ	❈	أَفْنَى الْقُرُونَ وَأَفْنَى كُلَّ ذِي عُمُرِ	48
فَنَجِّنَا مِنْ عَذَابِ الْمَوْقِفِ النَّكِدِ	❈	يَا رَبِّ إِنَّكَ ذُو عَفْوٍ وَمَغْفِرَةٍ	49
مَعَ النَّبِيِّينَ وَالْأَبْرَارِ فِي الْخُلْدِ	❈	وَاجْعَلْ إِلَى جَنَّةِ الْفِرْدَوْسِ مَوْئِلَنَا	50
مَنِ اهْتَدَى بِهُدَى رَبِّ الْعَالَمِينَ هُدِي	❈	سُبْحَانَ رَبِّكَ رَبِّ الْعِزِّ مِنْ مَلِكِ	51

46- And made death above creation, no refuge,

From it, nor escape to any support.

47- Death itself will die, and all will perish except,

The face of the Generous God, the eternal, the Independent.

48- He annihilated generations and every being with a lifespan,

Like the age of Noah and Luqman, the brother of Labad.

49- O Lord, You are of forgiveness and mercy,

So save us from the perilous agonizing stand.

50- And make our abode the Garden of Paradise,

With the prophets and the righteous in eternity.

51- Glorified is your Lord, the Lord of Majesty, as a Ruler,

Whoever guided by the Lord of the Worlds' direction is saved.

References

Al-Dhahabi, Shams al-Din Abu `Abd Allah Muhammad ibn Ahmad ibn
`Uthman.

- **Tārīkh al-Islām wa Wafayāt al-Mashāhīr wa al-A`lām**. Edited by Dr.
  Bashar `Awwad Ma`ruf. Beirut: Dar al-Gharb al-Islami, 1st edition,
  1424 H / 2003 CE.

- **Siyar A`lām al-Nubalāﷺ**. Edited by a group of scholars under the
  supervision of Sheikh Shu`aib Al-Arnaﷺut. Introduction by
  Bashar `Awwad Ma`ruf. Beirut: Muﷺassasat al-Risalah, 3rd
  edition, 1405 H / 1985 CE.

- **Mīzān al-I`tidāl fi Naqd al-Rijāl**. Edited by `Ali Muhammad al-
  Bajawi. Beirut: Dar al-Ma`rifah, 1st edition, 1382 H / 1963 CE.

al-Isfahani, Abu Nu`aym Ahmad ibn `Abd Allah. **Ḥilyat al-Awliyā' wa
Ṭabaqāt al-Aṣfiyā'**. Cairo: Matba`at al-Sa`adah, 1394 H / 1974 CE.

Al-Jaylani, `Abd al-Qadir ibn Musa ibn `Abd Allah. **Al-Ghunya li Ṭālibī 'l-
Ḥaqq**. Edited by Abu `Abd al-Rahman Salah ibn Muhammad ibn
`Uwaydah. Beirut: Dar al-Kutub al-`Ilmiyyah, 1st edition, 1417 H / 1997
CE.

Al-Mustaﷺsimi, Muhammad ibn Aydamur. **Al-Durr al-Farid wa Bayt al-
Qasid**. Edited by Dr. Kamil Salman Al-Jubouri. Beirut: Dar al-Kutub al-
`Ilmiyyah, 1st edition, 1436 H / 2015 CE.

Al-Suyuti, Jalal al-Din Yusuf ibn TaghriBardi. **Al-Nujūm al-Zāhira fi Mulūk Misr wa al-Qāhira.** Cairo: Ministry of Culture and National Guidance, Dar al-Kutub, Egypt.

Ebstein, Michael. *"Dhū 'l-Nūn al-Miṣrī and Early Islamic Mysticism."* **Arabica,** vol. 61, 2014, pp. 559-612. Leiden: Brill.

Ibn `Asakir, Ali ibn al-Hasan ibn Hibat Allah. **Tārīkh Madīnat Dimashq.** Muhibb al-Din Abu Sa`id `Umar ibn Gharamah al-`Amrawi Ed. Beirut: Dar al-Fikr for Printing, Publishing and Distribution, 1415 H / 1995 CE.

Ibn al-Jawzi, Jamal al-Din Abu al-Faraj `Abd al-Rahman ibn `Ali. **Manāqib al-Imām Aḥmad.** Edited by Dr. `Abd Allah ibn `Abd al-Muhsin al-Turki. Dar Hijr, 2nd edition, 1409 H.

Ibn Hajar al-`Asqalani, Ahmad ibn `Ali. **Lisān al-Mīzān.** Edited by `Abd al-Fattah Abu Ghuddah. Beirut: Dar al-Bashair al-Islamiyyah, 1st edition, 2002 CE.

Ibn Khallikan, Shams al-Din Ahmad ibn Muhammad. **Wafayāt al-A`yān wa Anbāءاللَّهُ رَحَمَ Abnāءاللَّهُ رَحَمَ al-Zamān.** Edited by Ihsan Abbas. Beirut: Dar Sader.

Smith, M. *"Dhu 'l-Nūn, Abu 'l-Fayḍ".* In: **Encyclopaedia of Islam,** Second Edition, Edited by: P. Bearman, Th. Bianquis, C.E. Bosworth, E. van Donzel, W.P. Heinrichs.

Made in the USA
Coppell, TX
16 December 2024

42634713R00030